Sally
Snowman

Story by Annette Smith

Illustrations by Meredith Thomas

Sally is looking at the snow.

Here comes Sally.

"Look, Mum," said Sally.

"Here is a little snowman."

The sun is on

the little snowman.

"Mum! Mum!" said Sally.

"**Look** at my little snowman."

Mum is looking at

Sally's snowman.

"Come here, Sally," said Mum.

"Here is a big snowball."

"Look at the **big** snowman,"
said Sally.